ISBN 979-8-89587-604-6
Library of Congress Control Number: 2024925353

Written by: Brandy Doss
Edited by: Brittany Cherelle
Published by: Boss Lady Media

Table of Contents

Dedication

For my readers, I want to give you a special thank you for reading my book and I hope it is a resource that you may relate to for strength, courage and resilience. If you have endured molestation, mental abuse, verbal abuse, or oppression in any aspect of your life, the choice to move forward is yours. Remember, positivity gives life and negativity takes life.

INTRO

He Just Said I Was Beautiful

I can remember back to being around family and noticing a difference in their body language, conversation and interactions with me. I recall smiles that were carved more for interest of me physically than family love. I remember questioning my thoughts, actions, and making excuses like "Oh, they've been drinking." I thought that the first time I was fondled, touched, kissed on by family, that it was my fault. I started to ask myself, *what did I do?*

The next time when it happened by a different family member, I just could not understand why me? Then, I thought to myself, *Well I am a teenage parent*, which I'm sure made me lose the "perfect little girl" image. While growing up, I was an honor roll student and excelled in every

4

area of academics. I pursued excellence in everything I did for many reasons. First being, I am the oldest child, and I wanted my siblings to have a positive role model. Another reason was I could not afford to get in any more trouble after the pregnancy. I had to help my single mother of four and did not want to burden her anymore. I was the family peace maker, problem solver, listening ear and encourager no matter what was happening in my life. My mother never allowed slack in our home, but I never complained. She always provided our needs and wants.

The actions of the previous adult men that took advantage of me physically and emotionally affected my mental health. I grew up with a mindset that every man was interested in me sexually and thought I was beautiful. I'll be honest, I had a very arrogant (superiority or self-importance, excessively confident) behavior while contemplating who I was and who I was going to become. This led to me becoming not only an overachiever but an anxious overachiever. Definition: "The

Anxious Overachiever Mindset – It's like a double-edged sword, brings both impressive accomplishments and significant challenges. This mindset is often characterized by an insatiable thirst for success, a relentless drive to exceed expectations, and a constant search for validation through achievement." With this mindset and everything I was going through, I remember asking myself, *is this life even worth living?*

CHAPTER 1

Life Halt

The definition of halt is "A suspension of movement or activity, typically a temporary one." So, let's say I had a halt in this production called life. See, I was pregnant at the age of fifteen and gave birth to my first child just before my sixteenth birthday. After my first child, I ended up having a total of three children just after I was a quarter of a century! I heard people say, "This is a golden age." However, for me, it was about survival. The life halts that I experienced made it difficult and challenging to strive forward during the transition from teenage years to instant adulthood.

I had to endure gossip from every end—at school, church and from my family. My classmates' parents placed boundaries, guidelines and restrictions on their children associating with me. I just did not understand my life. I had one parent tell her daughter she could no longer be a friend to me because I was too grown, even though I was just a teenager. A few of my classmates had abortions during our sophomore and junior year but were not spoken of. Yet because my mistakes were in the public eye, I was ridiculed. Well, if you thought that was enough, don't leave my family out of this picture-perfect event! My family called a meeting, and several individuals came in from out of town just to see me! In the living room was a circle formed of aunties and uncles with me in the center, and everyone had an opportunity to give suggestions, advice or scrutiny. I mentally could not comprehend why this was being done. However, I knew everyone loved me and desired the best for my life. They expressed all my accomplishments, success in academics and scholarships that would be affected by my current life decision. However, I believed that the correct thing to do was not kill my baby, to marry the baby's father and to abide by the bible and religious leaders. Many people did not know that a baby to me was someone I could love, and they would love me. As an adult now I understand the psychological changes and the "why" behind my mindset at that time.

I missed quite a bit of school, but thankfully I was able to do makeup classes over summer break at home. Typically, this was not an allowed regulation in schools, but I received an exception due to my circumstances. This exception put me on the path to graduate from high school on schedule. Although there were other struggles that made me eventually remove myself from traditional high school, I did achieve my General Educational Development Diploma. While in the GED program, I started working a full-time position in different industries like food, retail, and childcare. Whatever I could do to provide a living for my family.

Some might ask, "Why did you quit traditional high school?" See, I was on a mission to obtain additional education as quickly as possible to achieve my goals and not be a statistic! My first heartbeat was law, but when I dedicated my life to Christ, I was told by the church that I could not be a lawyer, stating, "I would have to jeopardize my commitment to be truthful."

Wow, at this point I redirected my mindset to the medical field. This just made sense to me, especially since two of my children have medical conditions. So, I was able to enroll in college for my Associate Degree in Applied Science for Health Care. During this transition, I started several certification programs, but I still did not feel complete on the inside. Once I realized that, I decided to continue my education while being a full-time mother.

I raised all my children with sacrifices that often led me to weeping, anguish and self-doubt. My kids now often state, "Momma, you have been in school ever since we can remember." While my children were younger, I completed several certifications and two degrees. I often paused in the process on this journey, but never gave up! I now hold a bachelor's degree in Health Care Management, a master's degree in Community Psychology and Sociology and have been in the medical field for over twenty years.

So, I know you're wondering "Where is the children's father? She hasn't said much about the children's father!" The children's father was present for a few years to the best of his abilities. We married at a very young age. I was only seventeen and he was eighteen. During this marriage, we were young adults working on finding our identity and understanding what marriage meant. The main reason for marrying young was based on the church, or should I state **RELIGION**. The leaders in the church made the Bible real plain on sex outside of marriage and that **HELL** was very real! Our families provided guidance, but the decision was ours to make. He decided to marry me when I informed him of the rules & regulations of the church. I expounded on how it was going to cause problems in our relationship if we didn't, and we truly desired to be together and raise our son together as a family. So, we started adulting in life and thought we understood!

Church was the focal point for me. Ministry was my foundation to being stable, consistent, balanced emotionally and a good woman. The ministry was also a negative in my relationship since it was religious not practical. Being reasonable was not often at the forefront of my mind. We are talking about balancing high school, marriage, friends, family, parenthood, and religion. I was at some type of church activity every day of the week. Monday was prayer night, Tuesday was Bible study, Wednesday – the young people's ministry, Thursday – choir rehearsal, Friday – pastoral teaching, Saturday – morning prayer, and on Sunday we had morning and evening worship.

This marriage lasted for some years, though we both had some growing up to do. The physical connection was there and the emotional was developing; however, our behavior towards each other mirrored what we saw in our upbringing.

This led to our separation by the time our second child was born, although we continued to have relations with one another, on and off. Then we had our third child. We were still married at this point, but the troubles in our marriage were becoming more and more present. A few months after our daughter was born, the father of my three children was no longer present in the home and the marriage was dissolved with no intentions of reconciliation.

CHAPTER 2

Contemplating Change

I have always strived for success and to be a better individual. However, the danger in overachieving is either a healthy perspective or an unhealthy mindset. Reality punched me in my gut in my late thirties. Let us take a stroll down memory lane.

Even in elementary school, I was the perfect child. Growing up I often heard accolades such as "perfect," "smart," "high achiever," "go getter," or "nerd" but in a positive manner. So, you get the point, right? However, the negatives in achieving and reaching goals with limited challenges are that it builds a perfectionist, overachiever, enough-is-never-enough mindset and "good enough" or criticism is self-evaluated very critically. It was rare to hear "you've done your

14

best." I can't recall my mother expressing how proud she was of me until adulthood, and my father was barely present during my childhood.

Growing up, my accomplishments became normal, which pressured me to achieve greater recognition or at least to feel appreciated. Criticism is a part of developmental maturity. However, criticism of my work screamed failure. To me, if I did not achieve my goals or desired grades, it would lead to sleepless nights and crying with knots in my stomach. See, I always received A's and B's—anything less was not good enough. I remember hearing my father's voice, "A 'C' is not good enough Brandy." So, when I made mistakes, I often had a negative mindset. Saying things like, "Come on, you know better" and "No excuses." Grace and mercy were not in my vocabulary when it pertained to myself, but I had no problem handing it out to others. My mentality continued in this mindset for years. However, when I got to college, I was rudely awakened with a new mindset and reality. That I am not PERFECT!

Now listen, somewhere in the back of my mind I knew I wasn't perfect. However, realizing it can make you want to slap yourself! The journey from elementary school to graduate school exceeded more years than I anticipated due to some of those life halts I was talking about. Including, but not limited to: being my mother's right hand, partnering with her in housework, chores, taking care of my three siblings while she worked two jobs. I juggled it all with this over achiever mindset!

During these years, I started to educate myself on me. I started to listen to professionals in healthcare, psychology and spiritual individuals. These individuals imparted a positive mindset, made me CONTEMPLATE CHANGE and put me on the journey to my holistic development.

According to Psychology Today, "The anxious overachiever: Holds themselves to over-the-top standards and then stews in self-criticism when they are not met with immediacy and precision. Perseverates over mistakes. Engages in toxic self-analysis and criticism. Has contingent self-esteem, relies on outside validation, accomplishments and accolades to fuel self-worth."

The freedom in understanding and moving forward in newness. I no longer consider or diagnose myself an Anxious Overachiever. I have applied the techniques to a new mindset through my education in psychology. The more I help others the more I am healed, delivered, and free to be my beautiful, flawed self! Growth is essential to life, and one must learn who they are to accept challenges, failures and move forward. It is all a part of our journey! My breakdown of the word G.R.O.W.T.H. means Goodness, Redemption, Openness, Work in progress, Truth and Healing. Ask yourself, "How can I start my G.R.O.W.T.H journey today?"

CHAPTER 3

Smiling & Hurting with Faith

I became a believer and joined church membership at age 17. My salvation was the only concern in the world at that time. I disconnected from family and friends unless they were a part of my faith, religion, and perspective. I isolated myself within the church world only. At that time, I was applying the scripture "Be careful for nothing" Philippians 4:6. by any means necessary. While I was growing in my faith, it was not always a clear revelation of the scriptures, therefore, I often just followed my leaders' teaching and input with no thought. I even separated from my mother at times, which stagnated our love for each other.

I was smiling and portrayed happiness while being igno-rant. This allowed me to be vulnerable in the church. I learned more negative things while being connected to a church and to the members than about God. I learned about homosexuality, condemnation, persecution, backbiting, slander, betrayal, and individuals with judgmental mindsets. The dangerous component was it affected me in my blindness spiritually.

The blindness intercepted my development mentally, spiritually, physically, and emotionally. My youthfulness, beauty and self-love were often suppressed, making sure not to be arrogant, haughty or vein. This was always connected to the Bible scriptures Proverbs 29:23 and Proverbs 16:18-20.

My wisdom, knowledge, understanding and positive, mature mindset activated in my late 20s. At this time, my mindset started to open from a fixed mindset to a growth mindset. I began to understand freedom versus bondage, or should I say removing the limited perspectives. One would believe that I was growing, I was learning and asking questions! My growth was a challenge in the natural world since the foundation in the spiritual world had been built. So, I started the journey of unlearning and relearning with the essential tools, skills, and techniques.

While on my life journey, education has always played a major role. While I was completing my master's degree in community psychology and sociology, I embraced my ability to have a holistic mindset. I started to understand the church structure, function, and application for living life. Christian living is not to enslave or entrap the mind, though often it happens. A Christian according to the Oxford Languages definition is "relating to or professing Christianity or its teachings." According to the Bible it is "someone whose behavior and heart reflects Jesus Christ."

Being a Christian helps to provide structure and guidance for everyday living. In every area of our lives, we need balance which leads to positive steps in our well-being. Living with balance includes self-care in our physical, psychological, emotional, social, spiritual and professional living according to Therapist Aid LLC. I am now living a holistic life with a positive, balanced mindset. I ask you, how are you living balanced or unbalanced? Where are you with your self-care?

Living Life on Purpose!!!

CHAPTER 4

Dating Again!

I will introduce my dating journey, first with sharing that I took courses online to make sure my heart was ready. I completed "Pray for Your Future Spouse" in 2021. This came with workbooks labeled "Worth the Work" and "Blind Spots Overlooked That Are Keeping You Single." The courses were provided by Jamal & Nathasha Miller, founders of The One University. This was enlightening, as it provided internal insight into who I am! The truth of the matter is we often misplace ourselves after death, trauma, grief, marriage, and childbirth.

I completed several lessons on love, marriage, grief, and remarrying through my Bible app to help me move forward with positive steps of well-being. After all the courses, training, and studying, it was still an eye-opener dating again after 20 years. I named this chapter of my life **Stupid**. Meaning, this season of my life reflects "having or showing a great lack of intelligence or common sense." This is the Oxford Languages definition of stupid.

Why call myself stupid? Yes, I have knowledge, skills, techniques, applications, and wisdom, but it still left room for me to find myself in a dark place, angry place, repenting place, and a place of emotional outburst, to paint the picture. I found myself unsuccessful a few times and then my mindset started to shift. I realized that not everyone I date is not marriage material, my future spouse or even my equal. I learned to embrace the moments and just live life! I know

God heard my heart when I prayed the first time, so now, I decided to enjoy living life!

Next, I decided to ask myself a few questions. "What do you desire to do now, Brandy?" "Do you truly desire marriage again?" "Do you desire to travel more?" "Brandy, are you okay with having a male friend and doing life with him without being married?" Yes, allow me to share openly and honestly!

I concluded that I want the abundant life promised to me according to the Bible. I do desire marriage again with traveling, learning, sharing, growing, caring, disagreeing in a positive respectful manner, etc. We are flawed humans and therefore, perfect is not reality. God created sex in the beginning though with standards and guidelines. How is it that we can forget the scriptures that provide meaning about marriage and not just sex? Scripture examples: 1 Corinthians 11:3, Ephesians 5:23, etc. Once I decided to start living with

Christ and not just for Christ, my new mindset reflected a question. **Are you living life abundantly? Are you living life above what you could even visualize?**

See, not marrying would place me in a position that I would not be content with at this point in my life. Marriage is more than **SEX!** Many people in the church have a narrow mindset, stating marriage is only desired for **SEX**. Always referring to single individuals, no matter of our perspective, life lived, former relationship, etc.

The benefits of sex according to WebMD are it boosts our immune system, improves sleep, boosts our mood, eases stress, and improves the health of the heart. Sex also relieves stress connected to the hormone called cortisol and releases other hormones in our bodies like endorphins. Sex offers natural pain relief and helps with menstrual health. Additional sex benefits include improved mental health and pelvic floor strengthening, to name a few.

CHAPTER 5

How Mr. Boaz Became Mr. Unpleasant!

First, let me share the good, better and best days in our marriage. Jimmy and I met after I had been divorced for seven years. We met while we were both working at Walmart. He first noticed me when I was in line for interviews. After we courted for six months, we decided not to let any more time pass and to get married. We had a successful, comfortable, exciting, fun, pleasant, loving relationship, with communication always the key component to our marriage. We were striving in ministry together and had no true financial burdens that we could not resolve. At the beginning, we both contributed to the union which allowed our union to grow quickly. He and I were living the life that we desired, after

27

both of us being former divorced individuals. Jimmy had been married twice before me and I had just been married once.

We blended our children without great struggles. He had one living adult son and I had three young children. We also welcomed his deceased daughter into our union. She was killed by an individual under the influence of alcohol. As a family, we went to the gravesite, introduced ourselves and shared a little about what we had learned about her life prior to death. We also prayed together while visiting with our deceased loved one.

When I state our union was SPECIAL, it was because he and I had both lived through some life, tests, tribulations and heartache from previous relationships. Jimmy and I had experience from a positive and negative perspective on how to move forward and not backward in a marriage to be healthy. He and I worked willingly with counsel to ensure our marriage was until death do us apart. We were living in overflow and abundance of blessings. We were able to donate vehicles, furnish individual's homes and assist others in different ways. We also went on two vacations yearly, one for the family and one for him and me to stay connected as a union. I am sharing what our marriage looked like before the shift.

There was an age difference between Jimmy & I, twenty-three years to be exact. When we met and started courting, I was twenty-five and he was forty-eight. The age difference was not our problem, it was the external family and friends that were concerned about our interactions moving forward. Jimmy was not a great talker, though in our marriage he believed in communicating with me. He and I traveled often by car and then started flying when driving was no longer convenient. We enjoyed driving to sightsee, exploring on the road trips while singing, seat dancing, talking and laughing out loud!

Listen, someone is saying our marriage sounded perfect. No, it was not perfect. Even though we were a blessed couple, God allowed us to go through our seasons. Our first argument was over him listening to the word of God and me wanting to listen to my gospel music at the same time. I remember stating, "I'm going to tell God on you!" He instantly became bothered, but then took a selah moment. He returned and stated, "I serve the same God, and I can tell him about you." We both started to laugh out loud and shook our heads! Moving forward, we learned how to incorporate the word and music at the same time. Basically, I am sharing how we became peaceful together at that time, not knowing the struggles we would face in about year thirteen of our marriage.

It is time to introduce how Mr. Boaz was forced to change mentally, spiritually, and physically that lead to me wanting to say, "I do not, after I said I do!" One day he was on the golf course playing golf and almost collapsed, which forced him to really investigate his health. We learned that he had hypertension first and then diabetes revealed itself not many years after. Jimmy's life before dedicating it to the lord was ungodly, like many of our lives used to be. The diagnosis led to medications that triggered side effects on his physical health. At first, he managed his health without my interference or suggestions. A year or so later, his health started changing in a negative manner that forced me to become involved.

The new diagnoses: pulmonary hypertension, right upper quadrant pain, right heart failure, acute respiratory failure, pneumonia due to the COVID-19 virus, chronic pain, impaired mobility and the one that challenged our faith was non-Hodgkin lymphoma (cancer). Wow is right, and now we were in a battle not just naturally, but spiritually. He was on twelve different medications. He had an allergic reaction to a couple of the medications, which led to damaging certain organs. This was a process to modify since corrections was an ongoing process until his death. The main medications prescribed at any given time for certain medical conditions affected him negatively. He was given medicines for hypertension, coronary artery disease and to rid fluid from his body connected to his heart.

Jimmy and I were now in a new marriage that involved several physicians, nurses, specialists and input on how to navigate our lives. Our marriage shifted overnight from our bedroom to sharing a room in the hospital at different intervals. We are now discussing a rapid change in our intimacy, communication, finances and his independence. First, our intimacy started to breakdown because we were not engaging sexually on a regular basis. We had to learn how to be intimate without becoming one physically for a season. This was challenging when we were embracing one another a couple of times per week before the shift in his health.

The next change was our communication, because he was tired of people prodding, sticking, testing and experimenting on him and he was fighting to maintain his independence, dignity and respect as a man. This led to financial adjustments, since we went from having multiple streams of income to losing one major stream. We eventually had to apply for disability to help supplement the multiple streams of income we once possessed. Now, he is struggling mentally with life adjustments all at one time.

I was challenged with being the only one working, continuing to maintain our home, landscape, business, children, bills, along with the new obligations. He was still maintaining what he could manage while battling with his health and mental change. We were living more on schedules, routines, checklists, medication lists, and doctor appointments, and no longer just living life without the cares of the world in front of us. This new marriage was working our patience, endurance, activities of daily living and wealth.

With all of this going on, one would think, *what else could possibly go wrong?* Well… his father dies, stepmother dies, and biological mother dies while we are going through these life adjustments! Yes, now death is weighing in on his mental health. Him and I had to go through the process of death, legal matters, grieving and family drama on top of every-thing else. Exhale, right? Wrong! Now our home gets shot up while we are sleeping! There were several bullets that penetrated our home, and one entered through our bedroom window. Allow me to illustrate clearly. If he or I was up going to the bathroom, the level of the bullet would have hit me in the chest and him around the neck. **BUT GOD!**

The repair process to the home was peaceful. Our insurance took care of everything, and it all went according to plan. It was repaired in a couple of weeks. My mindset was in the "what the hell is going on" kind of place. We are Christians, striving to live right but being attacked. The attack was meant for my middle son. Oh, did I mention this is the son that was shot and left to die? **BUT GOD!** The cowards that he got into it with from the streets decided to target his parents' home. Yes, I hear someone asking, were they arrested? To my knowledge, I do not know.

Jimmy and I continued battling with his health and life punches for several years. We both became different people. The doctors informed us three times during seven years that he was going to die and there was no more they could do with his health challenges. The attack on our home triggered his memories of his army days. I had to deal with him sleeping upstairs on the couch with a gun. He would lie with his hand hanging off the couch ready to pull the trigger. This went on for at least a week. The doctors later informed us that a certain type of specialist was needed, and a new facility was opening soon. Well, the new facility opened shortly after his death.

My entire household battled with a trauma mindset, triggers to acute stress, and had to readjust mentally with a holistic mindset. We all processed the acute stress individually and as a family with pastoral guidance and counsel. The healing journey mentally is ongoing until death, but managing and learning how to be victorious mentally is achieved!

CHAPTER 6

Living Through Breast Cancer

I am alive and striving to be the better me after another level of trauma. We will call this trauma the Breast Cancer Attack! My late husband died January of 2021 after a marriage of almost nineteen years. Allow me to remind you that his health was attacked physically and mentally for the last seven years of our marriage. The attack on his health placed an attack on my mental state at that time. I did not think that the stress, challenges, changes, and unknown circumstances in my marriage were activating internal unhealthy cell activity in my body.

The time that I was committed to caring for my husband was combined with me still being a parent of four, completing my master's degree in community psychology and sociology, preaching, teaching and building a business. **OH YES**, I was still working a natural job full-time for most of the last four years of out the seven. I then realized it was becoming overwhelming and I went to part-time work in health care. I have been in health care for twenty-one years and counting.

My late husband had multiple health attacks that rendered him not being able to do activities of daily living. His heart desires were challenged and affected by his mental health. Because my husband was a STRONG SOLDIER and the MAN of God that he was, we applied the spiritual more than the natural. However, we exhausted all natural remedies, medications, and procedures/surgeries that would extend life without him being a walking pin cushion or guinea pig. The doctors had one last opportunity, though the resource was not available prior to his death. I received a letter of his approval for care under a new specialty connected to neurology a few months after his death. This drove my mentality at that time from knowing where my life was heading to uncertainty. (Deep Breathing) (Exhale).

At this time, I also was connected to JP Productions and had appeared in their Christian films since 2020. I had wanted to do a movie of my life for some time, though life was coming at me like the wind from a tornado. When I finally decided to speak it into existence, my spouse's health was declining, and my finances had changed. A couple of years later, I am ready once again to place action behind things I spoke into existence, yet I am attacked!

It is the fall of 2022, and I received a diagnosis of breast cancer! Let me redirect your mind to my late spouse who died January of 2021. I was his wife, caregiver, mental support and prayer warrior daily for the entire marriage, though mainly the last seven years. Yes, my faith was tested and yes, I did fall short of believing God at times. However, I am excited because my diagnosis came with good news!! The good news was connected to everything I had been doing to help me while helping others, mainly my late spouse. I had changed our eating habits in the last seven years of my late spouse's life, which was a benefit for my health. I had started working out intensely by jogging, walking up to eight miles per day, weightlifting, boxing, hill climbing and dancing to help myself mentally, physically and spiritually. I had started taking vitamins, drinking special teas and was religious about staying on course. Therefore, when my care team and breast cancer physician met with me, it was about **living and not dying**! My physician stated, "You have been proactive in your health, which is a positive with any type of cancer." Yes, I faithfully completed preventive care appointments starting at the age of fifteen. This was primarily due to being a mother at such a young age.

My diagnosis was DCIS (ductal carcinoma in situ) and the stage was 0-1. The choices we discussed to correct this were lumpectomy with radiation, hormonal therapy, and mastectomy, which is the removal of the complete breast.

Chemotherapy was not an option for the degree of cancer I had due to several factors with being healthy, active, never smoked, or consumed alcohol or drugs. Also, that all the genetic testing done was **negative**! After completing additional special bloodwork and breast examinations, the best possible explanation of this diagnosis for me was connected to my internalized stress and former trauma.

According to the Merriam-Webster Dictionary, **trauma** is "An injury (such as a wound) to a living tissue caused by an extrinsic agent, A disordered psychic or behavioral state resulting from severe mental or emotional stress or physical injury." "An emotional upset, or an agent, force, or mechanism that causes trauma."

The initial plan was removal of the lump (lumpectomy) and radiation with hormone therapy. I declined hormone therapy and inquired about natural supplements that work in this diagnosis. Though now a test is needed to be done to see if I qualified for radiation. I had the testing done for radiation and it returned 50/50 it may benefit, or it may not benefit, and because of that radiation was a no go for me, according to my specialist. She stated the positives and negatives of having radiation and why it was no longer just being done without testing first. I did have the lump removed and we thought it was resolved at that time. However when I went for a follow-up after a few months, we realized that out of the four quadrants of the breast, very small particles of the same diagnosis were seen in two quadrants. **Exhale!!** A new plan to go forward now!! The first surgery was completed, and I was moving on to the next couple of surgeries to correct the abnormal activity in that breast. I had a total of six surgeries/procedures, though combined into three.

My journey was lumpectomy, lymph node biopsies, partial mastectomy, mastectomy (removal of complete breast), tissue expander, then a breast reconstruction with breast augmentation. I started my vitamin supplement that was in place of the hormonal therapy at the time of the diagnosis. My physician did her research on the supplement and gave the approval for me to take it along with staying active and being mindful of my eating style.

The breast cancer was **eradicated**, and I continued to follow my care with preventive appointments, seeing my specialist and plastic surgeon as scheduled. The doctors were amazed during the entire journey with how well everything went and how well my recovery went after every procedure/surgery.

**** Special Note*** Prayer covered me and carried me the whole time! The physical was not the greatest challenge for me, it was the mental! I had to learn how to live with a new body, mind, soul and spirit!! The benefit for me was that during the process, I was still seeing my mental health clients via tele mental health. I had a few breast cancer clients that had survived and were beautifully healed physically and were acknowledging the trauma that came from their former breast cancer. Helping others gave me the strength to want

to keep living and not quit!

CHAPTER 7

The Healing

The journey to my healing was orchestrated in segments and departments, with an analytical mindset. The more I see sickness, mental battles, and hope lost in others, the more I become driven to live. Exercising gives me life, literally! In psychology, exercising can be equivalent to an antidepressant, when properly implemented in daily living.

"We found that doing 150 minutes each week of various types of physical activity, such as brisk walking, lifting weights and yoga, significantly reduces depression, anxiety, and psychological distress, compared to usual care, such as medications," says Dr. Ben Singh in Medical News Today.

I started exercising more frequently when my late husband's health was attacked. I began walking a minimum of four miles per day. My exercising routines consist of jogging, sprints, weightlifting, hill climbing, yoga and Pilates. Well, laugh out loud, did I not mention boxing and dancing? Dancing is very therapeutic and exhilarating for me! I applied every tool and adaptive skill to help myself. I utilize two applications on my iPhone for support. My healing process involved prayer, church fellowship and continual education. I began educating myself in self-care, healthcare, psychology, finances, etc. I have obtained and exceeded five certifications and unlimited certificates. I have accomplished an associate, bachelor's, and master's degree that have equipped me to live life more abundantly!

I learned how to apply boundaries for myself, family, and friends. I learned positivity gives order to have life and that negativity removes life. The most fulfilling goal toward my healing was helping others in their time of need. Some examples are: furnishing other's homes, giving away vehicles, paying bills, and providing food and transportation. I share these things to express my gratitude for being an able vessel.

I recall my first-born son and I walking home with groceries

in a red wagon and him believing we were on an adventure!

The times the government system was a resource and shame

followed. Allow me to explain. I grew up in a household

where my mother worked two jobs at a time during my

school years. I was the oldest child; therefore, I was my

mother's support while maintaining my grades and working

a part-time job from fourteen years old. Though prior to that

I would babysit and iron clothes for the adults that would

out, so I could earn an income before I was of legal age to

work. For a season while raising my first born, we received

food stamps, Medicaid and WIC to help with survival. I

would not accept the money from them because I thought if

I take the money then I am at my lowest. I felt I would just

break. Yes, I am aware of pride and being prideful, though I

also recall dignity and self-respect, and I had to remind my-

self that I was able to do better! I remember talking to myself as a teen, stating government help is a form of slavery and I will not be trapped and not able to grow. Therefore, I recall speaking negative to myself until I made changes. I too worked multiple jobs to raise my children while going to school, because mentally, getting government support should be a stepping stone digging up the dirt to rise to higher ground.

My dad was on another level mentally. I recall my dad's input about government help, and it was not positive. The more income I would make the more the government would take or decrease what they were supporting my household with.

I am grateful for healing, deliverance, being whole and no longer broken. I love being able to love! Life cycles in seasons, going through a process, coming out of a process, or getting ready to enter a process no matter what cycle of life we are in. Remember, the mindset is ours to select!

CHAPTER 8

Brandy's Seasons

I first want to reiterate how the NIV Application Study Bible breaks down Ecclesiastes, chapter 3 verses 1-11. "A Time for Everything" I quote. In the commentary notes it expounds on timing, satisfaction, and life purpose. My life purpose is still coming forth. However, I am closer to understanding that my purpose is first about respecting God and viewing life as a gift.

My life journey has consisted of unanswered questions, times of overthinking, questioning my faith, questioning God's existence, and reminding myself why life matters. Not just for myself though, for those that are connected to me and those who depend on me to live life. Ecclesiastes 3:16

reads "And I saw something else under the sun: in the place of judgement – wickedness was there."

In the commentary notes on this verse it reflects on all the contradictions, but God is still in control. I correlate my life struggles, challenges, failures, successes and accomplishments to what God allows. This leads me to a perplexed mindset when speaking with God. Here's some of our conversations. **ME:** "God, do you not hear me?" **GOD:** "I hear you and that is why you **LIVED** through it all! Weeping may endure for a night though Joy comes in the morning!" **ME:** "God why the wait for this long?" **GOD:** "Be not without hope, Brandy." **ME:** "God why do I have to endure this hell/torment?" **GOD:** "Brandy, it is all connected to your life purpose. Why not you?"

I now must decide to live through it all or die now. Dying while living is real, naturally and spiritually. In a negative mindset death is the result. In a positive mindset growth with hope radiates in the darkness. Seasons in the natural comes with an expected timeline. However, it changes according to Earth, the axis, and orbital plane. Seasons in our lives come with an expectation of timing, but our mindsets can extend suffering or terminate a certain season on schedule to arrive.

Question: Have you ever gone through a situation in life where a timeline was given, though the plan of time has changed? Here are some examples: radiation, chemotherapy, marriage, childbirth, graduation, funeral arrangements, wedding, vacation.

I'm sure we all have, but in these situations, an **emotional mindset** causes you to react instead of responding. The emotional mind is used when feelings control a person's thoughts and behavior. They might act impulsively with little regard for consequences. What I've learned is that walking, running or crawling through seasons really doesn't matter. What matters is getting back up after every fall, shortcoming, down sitting or failure. I also learned that managing my emotions will keep me in a positive position mentally versus becoming emotional and acting out, harming someone with my mouth, regretting the choices I've made, and then apologizing. The greatest challenge with apologizing is working through letting it go from our photographic memory. Forgiveness is a process, though not forgiving others will cause more harm to yourself than the person being held hostage.

Additional Release from The Author

Behind Closed Doors are not just literal doors, but doors in my mind, heart, soul and spirit. Behind Closed Doors is the entrapment of my former broken self. Behind Closed Doors is my outpour from traumas such as child molestation and the mental challenges of not addressing it after the fact. The racism I experience in my teen years. I never understood the true depth of the hatred until I witnessed a race fight and heard the white men stating, "Kill the niggers" and saw guns drawn, baseball bats in people's hands, chains in people's hands as I stood there with fear for my life.

There were several challenges I endured within the place I viewed as a safe haven (church). I later learned that I had to be freed mentally from bondage, religion, and brokenness from within those walls. As I aged, the trauma continued:

My unfaithful first husband, middle son being shot, robbed, and left to die. My first born being shot while enjoying recreational activities. The birth of my daughter, the stressors in my marriage weighing heavily on my heart and mind. The bullets that entered my home while my family and I slept, to be awakened with my home shaken with slugs that pierced walls, windows, doors, and a mental shift for life.

One would believe that it stops here, right? **Wrong**, in my second marriage life was better. However, there was a transformation when his health was attacked and not only did he change, but it changed me. The journey of eighteen and a half years of marriage ended with death during our son's senior year of high school. I then had to fight to save my son's mental health during his transitional period of life into young adulthood, college and discovering who he is as a man without his father.

My late husband's death was not rapid. It was connected to preparatory and anticipatory grief. He battled with his health the last seven years of our marriage. The doctors stated he was going to die twice before the final time that they predicted during Covid. However, every time they stated death I interceded in prayer and had others praying with me for life extension. Finally, my late husband stated he was tired. Though every time he asked me if I was tired, I lied to keep him motivated to live life.

The shocking news later slapped me in the face that he had already been communicating with a male cousin, brother, and good friend about the process of death and his marriage. He and I finally discussed me being tired when I broke down in front of him crying. I was no longer able to deny that I was feeling overwhelmed, depleted, and defeated. It was at that time that he stated, "No I am tired," and he and I cried together, had our last meal together and attended our last worship service together. Two nights prior we made love for the last time. Once we had that discussion, he was gone at 3:00 pm Sunday afternoon. I later spoke with the ones he had spoken with about death and his marriage, and they informed me he held on because he stated, "My wife was not ready to let go." May I add this man of God taught me what love was and how to love! When working on him and trying to resuscitate him in our home, my mind was in a whirlwind, speaking with 9-1-1 on speaker phone yelling for them to come now, praying to God loudly and exhaling to not collapse myself from seeing life leave his body!

The warrior I am raised four children, endured hardship financially, mentally, verbally, and emotionally, now diagnosed with breast cancer years later. Though I was very healthy physically and never smoked, drank, or did drugs, it did not stop the attack of breast cancer leading to a mastectomy of a breast. I endured the physical recovery, but it was more about the mental recovery. I once believed I was untouchable because of all the good I'd done, helping others, sacrificing, but doing all I know that was right did no longer matter. Wow, what an eye-opener to see clearly that all my righteousness is not enough! I now understand others more with empathy, compassion and gratitude as I strive with positive steps for my wellbeing.

I am more than my trauma, brokenness, wounds, and scars, and see me in my healed self as beautifully flawed. I am the woman that I was created to be!

References

Lee, Kristen (2019) Are You a Healthy Achiever or Anxious Overachiever? Psychologytoday.com

Therapist Aid LLC (2015) The Wise Mind. TherapistAid.com

Schmidt, Nicole. Health & Sex, 9 Surprising Health Benefits of Sex. WebMD.com

Berman, Robby (2023) Is exercise more effective than medication for depression and anxiety? Medicalnewstoday.com

Merriam-webster.com/dictionary/trauma

Acknowledgements

First off, I give honor to God for life, health, strength and helping me in times of trouble.

To my momma, Jacquelyn McIntyre, I truly am thankful for you being the strong woman you are and my model in life. I watched you overcome life obstacles and not give up. Because of that, I continue to choose life and not give up.

To my late husband, James E. Doss Jr., I thank you for displaying what love was and how to expresses it until death parted us. You helped me understand what unconditional love means in a marriage.

To my awesome four children. To Christopher, QuWayin, Sheniah and Justin. All your faith, hope, trust and the strength you have seen in me kept me wanting to live even when I considered death. Many times, Sheniah, being my only daughter, would state, "Momma you know God hears you." This was a reminder for me to hold on to my faith in God. Each one of my children view me as super-woman, even when I wanted to give up or questioned God, but they never changed their view of me. I remained super-woman and for that I love them even more!

To my Auntie Beverly Hood, this woman is like a sister to me. She listened to me without condemnation, judgement, or a bias perspective. This woman is the reason why I lived through my teenage years. Her love was unconditional, spiritually and naturally.

I give honor to all the spiritual leaders in my life that encouraged, uplifted, inspired, imparted growth, and guidance into my life.

About the Author

Meet Brandy Doss, a former mental health clinician for American Behavioral Counseling and an ordained elder in ministry. Brandy holds a master's degree in Community Psychology and Sociology, a graduate certificate in Clinical and Counseling Studies, an associate degree in Applied Science, and a bachelor's degree in Health Care Management. She has also completed additional training in trauma, mental health, food functions of the brain, addictions, workplace violence, and communication with older adults.

Brandy is certified in the Montreal Cognitive Assessment (MOCA), Tele-mental Health Training (THTC) and has earned certificates from the NAACP Civil Rights & Advocacy Training Institute in Compassion Focus Therapy, Eating Disorders, and Non-suicidal Self Injury.

Brandy has served on many youth and women's ministries, volunteered at the Julian Center for Battered Women, and provided patient care in various medical fields for over eighteen years. She believes in humanistic therapy, which takes an integrated approach that emphasizes human potential, self-discovery, and free will. Brandy is also a holistic health coach, helping people achieve their health goals.

Brandy's positive attitude and untiring services have been recognized with awards such as the Brenda Gibson Spirit Award from the Sickle Cell Program. As an ordained elder, she teaches, preaches, and counsels individuals.

Special Information

I am grateful and appreciative for JP Productions & Boss Lady Media for producing, editing and publishing my live stage play "Behind Closed Doors" and my book "Behind Closed Doors."

Please find more information about
JP Productions/Boss Lady Media and
**How to purchase a DVD copy of the
Live Stage Play at the website below!**
www.bossladymed.com/behindcloseddoors

Thank you again to all my readers and those who supported the live stage play of "Behind Closed Doors" either in person or by **DVD purchase.**

Your support is appreciated, and I look forward to hearing how "Behind Closed Doors" has inspired, enlightened and encouraged you or someone you know. Comments are welcomed on website for book reviews/live stage play reviews.

Thank You,
-Brandy Doss

www.ingramcontent.com/pod-product-compliance
Lightning Source LLC
Chambersburg PA
CBHW051242120626
46547CB00014B/1759